CW00498971

The Gender-Neutral Baby Name Book

OVER 1,000 UNISEX, ANDROGYNOUS, NON-GENDER NAMES

Congratulations!

If you are reading this book, you are quite obviously starting your journey on the search for a baby name. There are many reasons to choose a gender-neutral or "unisex" name, and to help you on the process I am sharing the over 1,100 non-gender baby names I collected that I used when deciding on a name for my child. What you will notice however, is I did not include the:

- National origin
- "Meaning" or definition
- Religious context

Why you might ask? We live in a global world, and all names deserve to be celebrated. If a name speaks to you, and you feel that it fits the spirit of your child, you should not feel constrained by the "standards" of what society might impose or dictate is appropriate. Considering you might have purchased this book because it is non-gender baby names, you likely already know that! My point is that subconscious bias can sneak in, even with the best of us, so I felt it best to not add in. If you are really curious, I would suggest you look it up after you have selected a name.

To help you and your partner out (if you have one), I have check-boxes by each name. This was so helpful to me as I wanted the name selection for my child to be a thoughtful journey, and I could better keep track of my "short-list".

I also included a section for "notes & thoughts" after each Alphabetical grouping of names...you might be surprised how many new ideas you'll come up with! Different spellings, mixing in letters or sounds that have deep meaning to you, and more.

Please, use this book as a guide and a starting point. This is your journey with a new human life, and that is so special and exciting! There are no rules here, this is for you and your child.

Table of Contents:

- ☐ Addison
- ☐ Adina
- ☐ Adler
- ☐ Adria
- ☐ Adrian
- ☐ Adrian
- ☐ Adriel
- ☐ Aero
- ☐ Afton
- ☐ Aiden
- ☐ Aiken
- ☐ Ainsley
- ☐ Ainslie
- ☐ Airlie
- ☐ Al
- ☐ Alabama
- ☐ Albany
- ☐ Alby
- ☐ Aldus
- ☐ Alex
- ☐ Alexi
- ☐ Alexis
- ☐ Ali
- ☐ Alick
- ☐ Alix
- ☐ Allard
- ☐ Allie
- ☐ Ally
- ☐ Alvi
- ☐ Amara

- ☐ Amari
- ☐ America
- ☐ Americus
- ☐ Ames
- ☐ Amit
- ☐ Anan
- ☐ Anat
- ☐ Andi
- ☐ Andy
- ☐ Angel
- ☐ Ara
- ☐ Arden
- ☐ Aren
- ☐ Ari
- ☐ Arich
- ☐ Ariel
- ☐ Arien
- ☐ Aries
- ☐ Arion
- ☐ Arlo
- ☐ Arron
- ☐ Arrow
- ☐ Artemis
- ☐ Ascher
- ☐ Ash
- ☐ Ashby
- ☐ Asher
- ☐ Ashley
- ☐ Ashton
- ☐ Aspen

- [ ] Aubrey
- [ ] Auden
- [ ] August
- [ ] Avery
- [ ] Avis

Notes & Thoughts

- [ ] Baden
- [ ] Bailey
- [ ] Baker
- [ ] Bane
- [ ] Barr
- [ ] Barret
- [ ] Barrett
- [ ] Bates
- [ ] Bay
- [ ] Bayle
- [ ] Beckett
- [ ] Beecher
- [ ] Belen
- [ ] Bell
- [ ] Bellamy
- [ ] Bennet
- [ ] Benning
- [ ] Bentley
- [ ] Berkley
- [ ] Bern
- [ ] Bernie
- [ ] Bertie
- [ ] Bevan
- [ ] Bijou
- [ ] Billie
- [ ] Binder
- [ ] Blaer
- [ ] Blaine
- [ ] Blair
- [ ] Blaire

- ☐ Blake
- ☐ Blakely
- ☐ Blanket
- ☐ Blythe
- ☐ Bo
- ☐ Bobbie
- ☐ Bobby
- ☐ Bodie
- ☐ Bowie
- ☐ Braddock
- ☐ Bradin
- ☐ Brady
- ☐ Bradyn
- ☐ Braiden
- ☐ Braidy
- ☐ Braith
- ☐ Brantley
- ☐ Brayden
- ☐ Braydon
- ☐ Brenner
- ☐ Brett
- ☐ Briar
- ☐ Brice
- ☐ Bridge
- ☐ Brier
- ☐ Briggs
- ☐ Brilliant
- ☐ Brinley
- ☐ Bristol
- ☐ Brit

- ☐ Britt
- ☐ Brockey
- ☐ Brocky
- ☐ Bronwyn
- ☐ Brook
- ☐ Brooke
- ☐ Brooklyn
- ☐ Bryn
- ☐ Brynn
- ☐ Bryton

Notes & Thoughts

- ☐ Cade
- ☐ Caden
- ☐ Cadence
- ☐ Caelan
- ☐ Cage
- ☐ Cagney
- ☐ Cal
- ☐ Caldwell
- ☐ Calgary
- ☐ Camden
- ☐ Camdyn
- ☐ Cameron
- ☐ Campbell
- ☐ Cande
- ☐ Cannan
- ☐ Carlen
- ☐ Carlin
- ☐ Carman
- ☐ Carmine
- ☐ Carol
- ☐ Carrigan
- ☐ Carrington
- ☐ Carroll
- ☐ Carson
- ☐ Carsyn
- ☐ Casey
- ☐ Cassidy
- ☐ Cassy
- ☐ Castel
- ☐ Cato

- ☐ Cedar
- ☐ Celyn
- ☐ Chance
- ☐ Chandler
- ☐ Channer
- ☐ Channing
- ☐ Chanter
- ☐ Chantry
- ☐ Charleston
- ☐ Charley
- ☐ Charli
- ☐ Charlie
- ☐ Chase
- ☐ Chelsey
- ☐ Chevis
- ☐ Chris
- ☐ Christmas
- ☐ Clay
- ☐ Cleo
- ☐ Coby
- ☐ Cody
- ☐ Colorado
- ☐ Conner
- ☐ Connery
- ☐ Cooper
- ☐ Corbin
- ☐ Corey
- ☐ Corin
- ☐ Courtney
- ☐ Crane

- ☐ Crimson
- ☐ Crosby
- ☐ Cruz
- ☐ Cullen
- ☐ Cyrille
- ☐ Cyrpus

Notes & Thoughts

- ☐ Dabney
- ☐ Dacey
- ☐ Dahl
- ☐ Dakota
- ☐ Dale
- ☐ Dallas
- ☐ Dallon
- ☐ Damian
- ☐ Dana
- ☐ Danner
- ☐ Danni
- ☐ Dannie
- ☐ Danny
- ☐ Darby
- ☐ Daryl
- ☐ Daveney
- ☐ Davide
- ☐ Davignon
- ☐ Davin
- ☐ Dawson
- ☐ Daylin
- ☐ Dayton
- ☐ Daytona
- ☐ Dee
- ☐ Delaney
- ☐ Delta
- ☐ Demi
- ☐ Denim
- ☐ Deniz
- ☐ Denny

- ☐ Denver
- ☐ Deon
- ☐ Derby
- ☐ Derring
- ☐ Desi
- ☐ Destry
- ☐ Deven
- ☐ Devin
- ☐ Devin
- ☐ Devo
- ☐ Devon
- ☐ Devyn
- ☐ Dian
- ☐ Dillan
- ☐ Dillion
- ☐ Dillon
- ☐ Dion
- ☐ Dominique
- ☐ Dorian
- ☐ Drew
- ☐ Dru
- ☐ Drury
- ☐ Dublin
- ☐ Dunne
- ☐ Dusty
- ☐ Dwyn
- ☐ Dylan
- ☐ Dyre

Notes & Thoughts

- ☐ Easton
- ☐ Echo
- ☐ Eddi
- ☐ Eddie
- ☐ Eddy
- ☐ Eden
- ☐ Edge
- ☐ Egypt
- ☐ Eike
- ☐ Eisa
- ☐ Eka
- ☐ Elan
- ☐ Eli
- ☐ Elian
- ☐ Elie
- ☐ Eliot
- ☐ Elliot
- ☐ Ellis
- ☐ Ellison
- ☐ Elvan
- ☐ Elvis
- ☐ Emerson
- ☐ Emery
- ☐ Emlen
- ☐ Emlyn
- ☐ Emory
- ☐ Ennis
- ☐ Erin
- ☐ Erron
- ☐ Erryn

- ☐ Eston
- ☐ Evan
- ☐ Even
- ☐ Ever
- ☐ Everest
- ☐ Evren
- ☐ Evrim
- ☐ Ezra

Notes & Thoughts

- ☐ Fabian
- ☐ Fable
- ☐ Falan
- ☐ Falcon
- ☐ Fallon
- ☐ Farah
- ☐ Farley
- ☐ Farmer
- ☐ Farren
- ☐ Faulkner
- ☐ Fergie
- ☐ Finlay
- ☐ Finley
- ☐ Finnegen
- ☐ Flanders
- ☐ Flannery
- ☐ Florian
- ☐ Forest
- ☐ Frances
- ☐ Francis
- ☐ Franki
- ☐ Frankie
- ☐ Freddi

Notes & Thoughts

- ☐ Gabbi
- ☐ Gabbie
- ☐ Gabby
- ☐ Gabi
- ☐ Gable
- ☐ Gabriel
- ☐ Gail
- ☐ Gamal
- ☐ Garan
- ☐ Garnet
- ☐ Gatlin
- ☐ Gaven
- ☐ Gavyn
- ☐ Gentry
- ☐ Gerry
- ☐ Gillian
- ☐ Glen
- ☐ Glenn
- ☐ Glyn
- ☐ Gomer
- ☐ Gray
- ☐ Grayson
- ☐ Greer
- ☐ Grey
- ☐ Gusty

Notes & Thoughts

- ☐ Hadar
- ☐ Hai
- ☐ Halen
- ☐ Haley
- ☐ Halo
- ☐ Hami
- ☐ Hani
- ☐ Hanne
- ☐ Happy
- ☐ Harding
- ☐ Harlan
- ☐ Harley
- ☐ Harlow
- ☐ Harper
- ☐ Harshal
- ☐ Hartley
- ☐ Haven
- ☐ Hayden
- ☐ Hayley
- ☐ Helgi
- ☐ Helle
- ☐ Hennie
- ☐ Henny
- ☐ Hero
- ☐ Hollace
- ☐ Holland
- ☐ Hopeton
- ☐ Horizon
- ☐ Hosni
- ☐ Hudson

Notes & Thoughts

- ☐ Ibis
- ☐ Ickett
- ☐ Indiana
- ☐ Indigo
- ☐ Indy
- ☐ Issy
- ☐ Ivory
- ☐ Izel

Notes & Thoughts

☐ Jace

☐ Jacey

☐ Jaci

☐ Jacki

☐ Jackie

☐ Jacky

☐ Jadyn

☐ Jaffe

☐ Jaiden

☐ Jaime

☐ Jaimen

☐ Jaimin

☐ Jain

☐ Jalen

☐ Jam

☐ Jamal

☐ Jamari

☐ Jame

☐ Jameson

☐ Jamie

☐ Jan

☐ January

☐ Janus

☐ Jarah

☐ Jay

☐ Jayce

☐ Jaycee

☐ Jayden

☐ Jaye

☐ Jaylin

- ☐ Jaymes
- ☐ Jean
- ☐ Jeren
- ☐ Jerri
- ☐ Jerrie
- ☐ Jerry
- ☐ Jersey
- ☐ Jesse
- ☐ Jian
- ☐ Jimi
- ☐ Jinan
- ☐ Jody
- ☐ Joe
- ☐ Joey
- ☐ Jojo
- ☐ Jonas
- ☐ Jordan
- ☐ Jordyn
- ☐ Jorryn
- ☐ Jory
- ☐ Joss
- ☐ Jourdain
- ☐ Journey
- ☐ Joyce
- ☐ Jules
- ☐ Julian
- ☐ Juniper
- ☐ Juno
- ☐ Justice

Notes & Thoughts

- ☐ Kade
- ☐ Kaden
- ☐ Kadin
- ☐ Kai
- ☐ Kail
- ☐ Kalin
- ☐ Kalyan
- ☐ Kameron
- ☐ Kami
- ☐ Kamon
- ☐ Kamron
- ☐ Kamryn
- ☐ Karam
- ☐ Karter
- ☐ Kasen
- ☐ Kasey
- ☐ Kassidy
- ☐ Kavi
- ☐ Kayce
- ☐ Kayin
- ☐ Keanu
- ☐ Keaton
- ☐ Keegan
- ☐ Keelan
- ☐ Keeley
- ☐ Kei
- ☐ Keiran
- ☐ Keith
- ☐ Kel
- ☐ Kelby

- ☐ Kelley
- ☐ Kelly
- ☐ Kelsea
- ☐ Kelsey
- ☐ Keltie
- ☐ Kelty
- ☐ Kendahl
- ☐ Kendall
- ☐ Kendi
- ☐ Kendix
- ☐ Kenley
- ☐ Kennedy
- ☐ Kensley
- ☐ Kenzie
- ☐ Keran
- ☐ Kern
- ☐ Kerr
- ☐ Kerry
- ☐ Kesley
- ☐ Kevin
- ☐ Kevyn
- ☐ Kiffen
- ☐ Kiley
- ☐ Killian
- ☐ Kimball
- ☐ Kin
- ☐ Kindall
- ☐ Kingsley
- ☐ Kinley
- ☐ Kinsley

- ☐ Kipp
- ☐ Kiran
- ☐ Kit
- ☐ Kitt
- ☐ Kodrell
- ☐ Kody
- ☐ Kolton
- ☐ Kory
- ☐ Kris
- ☐ Kumi
- ☐ Kylan
- ☐ Kyle
- ☐ Kyler
- ☐ Kyrie

Notes & Thoughts

- ☐ Lake
- ☐ Landry
- ☐ Lane
- ☐ Lang
- ☐ Langley
- ☐ Laran
- ☐ Larue
- ☐ Latyen
- ☐ Lauren
- ☐ Laurie
- ☐ Lave
- ☐ Lavern
- ☐ Layne
- ☐ Layton
- ☐ Leal
- ☐ Lee
- ☐ Leigh
- ☐ Lennon
- ☐ Lennox
- ☐ Lenny
- ☐ Lesley
- ☐ Leslie
- ☐ Lesly
- ☐ Leven
- ☐ Lex
- ☐ Lincoln
- ☐ Linden
- ☐ Lindley
- ☐ Lindsay
- ☐ Lindsey

- ☐ Lindy
- ☐ Linley
- ☐ Linwood
- ☐ Lion
- ☐ Lior
- ☐ Loba
- ☐ Locke
- ☐ Loe
- ☐ Loften
- ☐ Loften
- ☐ Logan
- ☐ Loge
- ☐ Loki
- ☐ Lolani
- ☐ London
- ☐ Lorand
- ☐ Lorant
- ☐ Loren
- ☐ Loreto
- ☐ Lorin
- ☐ Lou
- ☐ Louie
- ☐ Luca
- ☐ Luka
- ☐ Lumi
- ☐ Lundy
- ☐ Lux
- ☐ Lydon
- ☐ Lyndsey
- ☐ Lyric

Notes & Thoughts

- ☐ Macall
- ☐ Macaulay
- ☐ Maccaulay
- ☐ Macey
- ☐ Mackenzie
- ☐ Maclean
- ☐ Macrae
- ☐ Madan
- ☐ Madden
- ☐ Maddi
- ☐ Maddy
- ☐ Madison
- ☐ Madrid
- ☐ Maik
- ☐ Maine
- ☐ Malise
- ☐ Mallory
- ☐ Mandeep
- ☐ Manning
- ☐ Manny
- ☐ Mara
- ☐ Marage
- ☐ Mari
- ☐ Marjus
- ☐ Marka
- ☐ Marley
- ☐ Marlin
- ☐ Marlow
- ☐ Marlowe
- ☐ Marvel

- ☐ Mason
- ☐ Mato
- ☐ Mattie
- ☐ Max
- ☐ Maxwell
- ☐ Mckale
- ☐ Mckinley
- ☐ Memphis
- ☐ Mercer
- ☐ Meris
- ☐ Merit
- ☐ Merle
- ☐ Merrit
- ☐ Merritt
- ☐ Merton
- ☐ Meryl
- ☐ Messina
- ☐ Micah
- ☐ Micha
- ☐ Michael
- ☐ Michon
- ☐ Michone
- ☐ Mickey
- ☐ Micky
- ☐ Mikey
- ☐ Mikkel
- ☐ Milan
- ☐ Millan
- ☐ Miller
- ☐ Mills

- ☐ Milne
- ☐ Miner
- ☐ Minke
- ☐ Miracle
- ☐ Mischa
- ☐ Mo
- ☐ Mobley
- ☐ Moe
- ☐ Monroe
- ☐ Monrow
- ☐ Montana
- ☐ Moody
- ☐ Morgan
- ☐ Moriah
- ☐ Mose
- ☐ Murphey
- ☐ Murphy
- ☐ Myke
- ☐ Myles

Notes & Thoughts

- ☐ Nat
- ☐ Natine
- ☐ Natsu
- ☐ Nature
- ☐ Naveen
- ☐ Navy
- ☐ Neo
- ☐ Neriah
- ☐ Nevada
- ☐ Nevin
- ☐ Nico
- ☐ Niel
- ☐ Nika
- ☐ Nike
- ☐ Noa
- ☐ Noah
- ☐ Noel
- ☐ Nolan
- ☐ Noland
- ☐ Notin
- ☐ Nova
- ☐ November
- ☐ Nowlan
- ☐ Nowles
- ☐ Nox

Notes & Thoughts

- ☐ Oakes
- ☐ Oakley
- ☐ Oberson
- ☐ Ocean
- ☐ October
- ☐ Odell
- ☐ Ohio
- ☐ Oklahoma
- ☐ Olli
- ☐ Ollie
- ☐ Olly
- ☐ Oma
- ☐ Omega
- ☐ Ondrea
- ☐ Oran
- ☐ Ordell
- ☐ Orin
- ☐ Orion
- ☐ Orly
- ☐ Owen
- ☐ Oz
- ☐ Ozzy

Notes & Thoughts

- ☐ Padma
- ☐ Pagen
- ☐ Paige
- ☐ Painter
- ☐ Paisley
- ☐ Paley
- ☐ Pallas
- ☐ Paras
- ☐ Paris
- ☐ Park
- ☐ Parker
- ☐ Parkin
- ☐ Parley
- ☐ Parris
- ☐ Parry
- ☐ Parson
- ☐ Pascal
- ☐ Pascha
- ☐ Pasha
- ☐ Pat
- ☐ Paton
- ☐ Pattie
- ☐ Patton
- ☐ Patty
- ☐ Paxten
- ☐ Paxton
- ☐ Payson
- ☐ Payton
- ☐ Peeta
- ☐ Pemberly

- ☐ Perrin
- ☐ Perry
- ☐ Peyton
- ☐ Phoenix
- ☐ Pier
- ☐ Pierce
- ☐ Piers
- ☐ Ping
- ☐ Piper
- ☐ Pluto
- ☐ Poet
- ☐ Prairie
- ☐ Prentice
- ☐ Presley
- ☐ Preston
- ☐ Proctor
- ☐ Prosper
- ☐ Prudance
- ☐ Prudence
- ☐ Psalm
- ☐ Puma
- ☐ Purdie
- ☐ Purdy

Notes & Thoughts

- [ ] Quennel
- [ ] Quennell
- [ ] Quest
- [ ] Quin
- [ ] Quincy
- [ ] Quincy
- [ ] Quinlyn
- [ ] Quinlynn
- [ ] Quinn
- [ ] Quinne
- [ ] Qwin

Notes & Thoughts

- ☐ Rafferty
- ☐ Rain
- ☐ Raine
- ☐ Raleigh
- ☐ Ramsay
- ☐ Ramsey
- ☐ Randi
- ☐ Randy
- ☐ Rani
- ☐ Raphael
- ☐ Raven
- ☐ Ravid
- ☐ Ray
- ☐ Rayne
- ☐ Raz
- ☐ Read
- ☐ Reading
- ☐ Reagan
- ☐ Rebel
- ☐ Red
- ☐ Redell
- ☐ Reece
- ☐ Reed
- ☐ Reegan
- ☐ Reese
- ☐ Regan
- ☐ Reggie
- ☐ Rei
- ☐ Reid
- ☐ Reilly

- ☐ Remi
- ☐ Remington
- ☐ Remy
- ☐ Ren
- ☐ Rene
- ☐ Rennie
- ☐ Renny
- ☐ Rey
- ☐ Reyne
- ☐ Rhode
- ☐ Rhodes
- ☐ Rhodey
- ☐ Ricci
- ☐ Ricki
- ☐ Rider
- ☐ Rigg
- ☐ Riggs
- ☐ Rigny
- ☐ Riley
- ☐ Rio
- ☐ Ripley
- ☐ River
- ☐ Roan
- ☐ Robbi
- ☐ Robbie
- ☐ Robin
- ☐ Robyn
- ☐ Rogene
- ☐ Rohan
- ☐ Rollin

- [ ] Rome
- [ ] Romy
- [ ] Rondell
- [ ] Ronni
- [ ] Roper
- [ ] Rory
- [ ] Rowan
- [ ] Rowdy
- [ ] Rudo
- [ ] Rudy
- [ ] Rumer
- [ ] Rumor
- [ ] Rune
- [ ] Rusti
- [ ] Rusty
- [ ] Ryalan
- [ ] Ryan
- [ ] Ryder
- [ ] Rylan
- [ ] Ryland
- [ ] Rylee
- [ ] Rylie

Notes & Thoughts

- ☐ Sabah
- ☐ Sable
- ☐ Sabriel
- ☐ Sacha
- ☐ Sachet
- ☐ Sage
- ☐ Sailor
- ☐ Saint
- ☐ Sal
- ☐ Sam
- ☐ Saman
- ☐ Sammi
- ☐ Sammy
- ☐ Sandi
- ☐ Sarva
- ☐ Sasa
- ☐ Sasha
- ☐ Sasson
- ☐ Sawyer
- ☐ Saxen
- ☐ Saxon
- ☐ Saxton
- ☐ Sayer
- ☐ Saywer
- ☐ Scorpio
- ☐ Scout
- ☐ Sean
- ☐ Seath
- ☐ Seeley
- ☐ Sefton

- ☐ Selby
- ☐ Sequin
- ☐ Seri
- ☐ Sevan
- ☐ Shae
- ☐ Shahan
- ☐ Shan
- ☐ Shane
- ☐ Shani
- ☐ Shannon
- ☐ Shashi
- ☐ Shawn
- ☐ Shay
- ☐ Shaya
- ☐ Shayne
- ☐ Shelby
- ☐ Shelley
- ☐ Shelly
- ☐ Sheridan
- ☐ Shiloh
- ☐ Shoney
- ☐ Shun
- ☐ Sibley
- ☐ Sidney
- ☐ Sigi
- ☐ Simon
- ☐ Simone
- ☐ Siri
- ☐ Skate
- ☐ Skule

- ☐ Skye
- ☐ Skylar
- ☐ Skyler
- ☐ Sloan
- ☐ Sloane
- ☐ Solaris
- ☐ Sora
- ☐ Sothy
- ☐ Sparrow
- ☐ Spencer
- ☐ Spirit
- ☐ Springer
- ☐ Stacey
- ☐ Stacy
- ☐ Star
- ☐ Starlin
- ☐ Stellan
- ☐ Steph
- ☐ Stevie
- ☐ Stevie
- ☐ Storm
- ☐ Storm
- ☐ Stormy
- ☐ Story
- ☐ Sturla
- ☐ Sully
- ☐ Sunan
- ☐ Sung
- ☐ Sunny
- ☐ Sutton

- ☐ Sutton
- ☐ Sydney
- ☐ Sydnee
- ☐ Syler

Notes & Thoughts

- ☐ Tabor
- ☐ Tacey
- ☐ Tait
- ☐ Taite
- ☐ Tallis
- ☐ Tam
- ☐ Taman
- ☐ Tandy
- ☐ Tanner
- ☐ Tappen
- ☐ Tapper
- ☐ Taregan
- ☐ Tarin
- ☐ Tarlo
- ☐ Tate
- ☐ Tatum
- ☐ Taurus
- ☐ Tay
- ☐ Tayden
- ☐ Taylor
- ☐ Tayte
- ☐ Tayten
- ☐ Teagan
- ☐ Teal
- ☐ Temple
- ☐ Terran
- ☐ Terri
- ☐ Terrian
- ☐ Terris
- ☐ Tevin

- ☐ Tex
- ☐ Thady
- ☐ Thane
- ☐ Theo
- ☐ Theron
- ☐ Thono
- ☐ Tia
- ☐ Tibby
- ☐ Tibone
- ☐ Tierney
- ☐ Tiger
- ☐ Timber
- ☐ Tip
- ☐ Toan
- ☐ Tobin
- ☐ Toby
- ☐ Tolliver
- ☐ Tomi
- ☐ Tommi
- ☐ Toni
- ☐ Tonie
- ☐ Tony
- ☐ Topper
- ☐ Torrance
- ☐ Torrel
- ☐ Torrin
- ☐ Tory
- ☐ Tracey
- ☐ Tracy
- ☐ Trapper

- ☐ Treat
- ☐ Trenton
- ☐ Trevon
- ☐ Tribly
- ☐ Trilby
- ☐ Trinity
- ☐ Tristan
- ☐ Tucker
- ☐ Tully
- ☐ Twilight
- ☐ Ty
- ☐ Tyler
- ☐ Tyne
- ☐ Tyree
- ☐ Tyrique

Notes & Thoughts

- ☐ Ulli
- ☐ Unique
- ☐ Urban
- ☐ Utah
- ☐ Vahn
- ☐ Vail
- ☐ Val
- ☐ Valor
- ☐ Vasha
- ☐ Vaughn
- ☐ Veda
- ☐ Venni
- ☐ Vic
- ☐ Vick
- ☐ Vicky
- ☐ Vine
- ☐ Virgo
- ☐ Viv
- ☐ Von
- ☐ Vonte
- ☐ Voss
- ☐ Vox

Notes & Thoughts

- ☐ Wallace
- ☐ Wallis
- ☐ Waverly
- ☐ Weaver
- ☐ Wednesday
- ☐ Wei
- ☐ Wen
- ☐ Weslan
- ☐ Wesley
- ☐ West
- ☐ Whitley
- ☐ Whitney
- ☐ Wickham
- ☐ Wilder
- ☐ Wiley
- ☐ Willie
- ☐ Willow
- ☐ Willy
- ☐ Wilmet
- ☐ Winter
- ☐ Winter
- ☐ Wisdom
- ☐ Wobbe
- ☐ Wook
- ☐ Wren
- ☐ Wylie
- ☐ Wynn
- ☐ Wynne
- ☐ Wyome
- ☐ Wyoming

Notes & Thoughts

- ☐ Xanadu
- ☐ Xander
- ☐ Xandy
- ☐ Xannon
- ☐ Xerxes
- ☐ Xing
- ☐ Yafe
- ☐ Yage
- ☐ Yale
- ☐ Yancy
- ☐ Yank
- ☐ Yannic
- ☐ Yannick
- ☐ Yarden
- ☐ Yardley
- ☐ Yildiz
- ☐ Yogi
- ☐ Yoshi
- ☐ Young
- ☐ Yule
- ☐ Yun

Notes & Thoughts

- ☐ Zaiden
- ☐ Zaire
- ☐ Zale
- ☐ Zan
- ☐ Zane
- ☐ Zara
- ☐ Zasha
- ☐ Zeal
- ☐ Zealand
- ☐ Zenith
- ☐ Zenon
- ☐ Zephyr
- ☐ Zephyr
- ☐ Zeta
- ☐ Zion
- ☐ Ziven
- ☐ Zoan
- ☐ Zody
- ☐ Zody
- ☐ Zuma

Notes & Thoughts

Printed in Great Britain
by Amazon

40858892R00051